12 CHEFS WHO CHANGED THE WORLD

by Jamie Kallio

12 STORY LIBRARY
MORE TO EXPLORE

www.12StoryLibrary.com

12-Story Library is an imprint of Bookstaves.

Photographs ©: PictureLux/Alamy, cover, 1; Anders Carlsson/CC2.0, 4; Kent Wang/CC2.0, 5; John Mathew Smith/CC2.0, 6; Mathew G. Bisanz/CC3.0, 7; Lynn Gilbert/CC4.0, 7; PD, 8; Calton/CC3.0, 9; Meal Makeover Moms/CC2.0, 9; National Endowment for the Humanities/PD, 9; Joe Seer/Shutterstock.com, 10; PD, 11; Foodista/CC2.0, 11; ZUMA Press Inc/Alamy, 12; City Foodsters/CC2.0, 13; Kathy Hutchins/Shutterstock.com, 14; 1000Photography/Shutterstock.com, 15; Mirrorpix/Alamy, 16; Roland Tanglao/CC2.0, 17; CSU Archives/Alamy, 18; Bill Golladay/CC4.0, 19; Kathy Hutchins/Shutterstock.com, 20; iHeartsy-Music/PD, 21; kai hecker/Shutterstock.com, 22; Chuck Kennedy/PD, 23; Leonard Zhukovsky/Shutterstock.com, 24; H. Michael Miley/CC2.0, 25; Roderick Eime/CC2.0, 26; Edsel Little/CC2.0, 27; Dov Harrington/CC2.0, 28; s_bukley/Shutterstock.com, 29

ISBN
9781632357151 (hardcover)
9781632358240 (paperback)
9781645820031 (ebook)

Library of Congress Control Number: 2019938654

Printed in the United States of America
July 2019

About the Cover
Julia Child in 1988.

Table of Contents

1 Magnus Nilsson: Raw Moose Heart on the Menu

Magnus Nilsson is a Swedish chef. He was born in 1983 in Jämtland, a county in the middle of Sweden. He remembers slicing cucumbers with his grandmother when he was four years old. He later went to cooking school and worked in restaurants in France. In 2008, Nilsson took over a small restaurant called Fäviken in a remote area of Sweden. Today it's known as one of the best restaurants in the world.

Nilsson cooks new wave Nordic food. He hunts, fishes, and uses local ingredients. The dishes are creative and can seem strange. Diners have been served wild trout in pig's blood, pieces of raw moose heart, and cake made of pine tree bark.

Magnus Nilsson and one of his creative dishes: duck with onion, green juniper berries, sprouted grains, and a raw mussel.

Nilsson is also an author. *The Nordic Cookbook*, published in 2015, contains 700 recipes he collected from the Nordic region. There are recipes from Denmark, Finland, Iceland, Norway, Sweden, and the Faroe Islands. *The Nordic*

2016

Year when Fäviken won two Michelin stars

- Fäviken is in an old barn. It seats only 24 people.
- People wait up to a year for a reservation.
- The restaurant is so remote that some visitors spend the night in small rooms upstairs.

Baking Book came out in 2018. It has 450 traditional recipes for Nordic pastries, breads, cookies, and cakes.

Many restaurant critics and food writers have made the long trek to Fäviken. Nilsson has also been on TV. He was featured in the PBS series *The Mind of a Chef* and the Netflix series *Chef's Table*.

Nilsson's restaurant Fäviken in Sweden.

MICHELIN STARS

Awarding Michelin stars is a way to rate restaurants. It was started by the *Michelin Guide* in 1926. Restaurants work very hard to earn star status. Stars are given for the quality of the food, the chef's mastery, the ingredients used, and how dishes are presented. Michelin stars can make a restaurant famous overnight.

2

Julia Child: Fun and Fearless

Julia Child in 1994.

Julia Child was born in California in 1912. When she died in 2004, she was 92 years old. She once said her long life was due to eating a lot of red meat.

Child grew up eating frozen dinners. In 1946, she married an American diplomat. They lived in Paris for five years. Child attended the famous Paris cooking school Le Cordon Bleu. She later cowrote a cookbook called *Mastering the Art of French Cooking*. Child wanted to make French recipes easy for Americans to cook. One of her best-known recipes is for beef bourguignon.

In 1963, Child began filming a cooking show, *The French Chef*. She was one of the first chefs to host a TV cooking show. She taught audiences that mistakes were part of learning. She demonstrated this when she couldn't flip a potato pancake on live TV. Child changed the way Americans cooked and ate.

JULIA CHILD, SPY

During World War II, Julia Child joined the Office of Strategic Services (OSS). This organization would later become the Central Intelligence Agency (CIA). She worked under the OSS Director. She helped develop a shark repellent that kept naval officers and equipment safe in the ocean.

Child's kitchen on display at the Smithsonian's National Museum of American History.

Child in her kitchen in 1978.

96

Number of PBS TV stations that broadcast *The French Chef*

- *The French Chef* was one of America's first cooking shows.
- Child won a Peabody Award in 1965 and an Emmy Award in 1966.
- She went on to film more cooking shows including *Julia Child and Company*, *Julia Child and More Company*, and *Dinner at Julia's.*

3

Alice Waters: Fresh and Local

Alice Waters is a chef and social activist. She owns the restaurant Chez Panisse in Berkeley, California. Waters was born in 1944 in New Jersey. Her parents kept a victory garden.

During college, Waters traveled to France. She loved the way food tasted there. She admired a restaurant's fresh, local ingredients. In 1971, she opened Chez Panisse. She did not have formal training as a chef.

Waters wanted to serve food made with only local ingredients. Her menu included farm-raised fresh duck instead of frozen. She formed relationships with local growers. She started what is now called the farm-to-table revolution. Waters has long been a supporter of the Slow Food movement. The movement is against unhealthy fast food.

In 1995, Waters started the Edible Schoolyard program. She planted a garden on a local school's property and taught students about healthy eating. In 1996, she founded the Chez Panisse Foundation to fund more schoolyard gardens. Today there are thousands of locations in the Edible Schoolyard network.

Waters and her restaurant have won several James Beard awards. In 1992, Chez Panisse was named Outstanding Restaurant and Waters

Alice Waters in 2015.

Restaurant Chez Panisse and an Edible Schoolyard garden.

was named Outstanding Chef. Waters was the first woman to win that award. In 2004, Waters won the Humanitarian of the Year Award. In 2004, the Beard Foundation gave her the Lifetime Achievement Award.

PRISON GARDENS

Waters works with the Horticulture Project at the San Francisco County Jail. The Garden Project trains inmates to organize and maintain a garden. The program helps inmates give back to society.

2015

Year when Alice Waters won the National Humanities Medal

- Waters believes that eating is a political act.
- She thinks that social justice and positive change can start at the table.
- She was given the medal by President Barack Obama.

4 Ina Garten: Hungry for Flavor

Ina Garten was born in 1948 in Connecticut. Like many American kids in the 1950s, she grew up eating bland food. She wanted to cook because she craved flavor. But her mother thought she should concentrate on homework and school.

Garten started to cook after she got married. She and her husband, Jeffrey, went on a four-month camping trip in France. Garten fell in love with the food there. It was full of flavors. Garten learned that good food is about good ingredients. Later, Garten and Jeffrey moved to Washington, DC. She got a job with the Office of Management and Budget (OMB). She started trying recipes from cookbooks by Julia Child.

Ina Garten with her husband Jeffrey at the Daytime Emmy Awards in 2013.

In 1978, Garten left her government job. She bought a small specialty food store in the Hamptons on Long Island, New York. The store was called Barefoot Contessa. It was named after an old movie. The store was only 400 square feet (37.2 sq m). Garten grew it to 3,000 square feet (278.7 sq m). She cooked most of the food herself.

In 1996, Garten sold the store to her employees. In 1999, she wrote her first cookbook, *The Barefoot*

Haricot Verte Salad from Garten's 2013 cookbook.

Contessa Cookbook. She wanted regular people to learn how to cook tasty food. Her recipes used familiar ingredients. Her warm, earthy style attracted a wide audience. The book became a best seller. Two years later, the Food Network offered Garten her own show. Millions of viewers tuned in to *The Barefoot Contessa*. So far, Garten has won three daytime Emmy awards and three James Beard awards.

Garten has published 11 cookbooks. More than 12 million copies are in print. Garten believes that cooking leads to happiness.

1.6 million

Number of Ina Garten's Instagram followers

- Garten's simple but elegant recipes have made her very popular.
- Although Garten is famous, she doesn't endorse products.
- She has never watched herself on TV.

5 Dominique Crenn: The Chef Who Writes Poetry

Dominique Crenn in 2013.

Dominique Crenn was born in 1965. She grew up in Versailles, France. Crenn's mother taught her about cooking. Her father gave her a love of art. Her family appreciated fine dining. They often went together to the best restaurants in the area.

Crenn moved to San Francisco in her twenties. She studied to be a chef. She worked in restaurant kitchens run by famous chefs and learned from them, too.

Her cooking skills drew attention. She spent a year in Indonesia, then returned to California. In 2011, she opened her own restaurant, Atelier Crenn. Atelier is French for workshop.

Crenn combines her love of art with her cooking. Her food is called modernist fine-French cuisine. Meals might be grilled local abalone, egg jam, and oyster-scented cream. The menu at Atelier Crenn is written like a poem. In 2013, Atelier Crenn won two Michelin stars. In 2018, it won another. This made Crenn the first female chef in America to win three Michelin stars.

Crenn was featured on Season 2 of the Netflix series *Chef's Table.* Her first cookbook, *Atelier Crenn: Metamorphosis of Taste*, was published in 2015. Crenn believes that a chef's first job is to feed people.

Course #10:
"Walking deep in the woods, as the earth might have something to spare."
– mushroom, pine, and pumpernickel.

5

Number of woman-run Michelin 3-star restaurants in the world

- Along with her Michelin stars, Crenn has a 2018 James Beard Award for Best Chef: West.
- Crenn hopes her fame will help other women in the male-dominated world of fine dining.
- In 2018, Crenn hosted a dinner series called "The Women of Food." It featured internationally acclaimed female chefs from across the United States.

TREES FOR HAITI

When Hurricane Matthew struck Haiti in 2016, it destroyed many crops and farms. In 2017, Dominique Crenn and another chef started the Root Project. They hope to plant more than a million coffee and cacao trees in Haiti, working alongside Haitian chefs and farmers.

6 Giada De Laurentiis: From New Kid to Favorite Chef

Giada De Laurentiis in 2015.

Giada De Laurentiis was born in Rome, Italy, in 1970. She and her family moved to the United States when she was seven. They settled in Los Angeles. De Laurentiis didn't speak English, and she was bullied by some of her classmates. So instead of hanging out with friends, she turned to her family. Her grandfather, Dino De Laurentiis, was a famous movie producer. He had a restaurant called DDL Foodshow. Giada liked spending time there.

After college, De Laurentiis moved to Paris. She studied cooking at Le Cordon Bleu. She specialized in cuisine and patisserie. Returning to Los Angeles, she worked as a caterer. Then she wrote an article for *Food & Wine* magazine about her family's traditional Sunday dinners. One of the people who read it was an executive with the Food Network. By 2003, De Laurentiis was hosting her own TV cooking show, *Everyday Italian*. Her friendly personality made her a fan favorite. Her food is modern Italian dishes that are delicious and healthy. In 2008, De Laurentiis won a daytime Emmy Award.

De Laurentiis has written nine best-selling cookbooks and produced

Restaurant Giada is in the Cromwell Hotel on the famous Las Vegas strip.

THINK ABOUT IT

Giada De Laurentiis comes from a family with many food traditions. What are some traditional foods in your own family? What kinds of food do you eat on holidays or for religious ceremonies?

8

Number of children's books De Laurentiis has written

- De Laurentiis is writing a series called *Recipe for Adventure.*
- In the series, two children named Alfie and Emilia travel to famous food cities around the world.
- De Laurentiis is an advocate for children's cancer research.

eight cooking shows including *Giada's Weekend Getaways* and *Giada at Home*. In 2014, she opened the restaurant Giada on the Las Vegas Strip. She was the first woman to own a restaurant there.

7 Madhur Jaffrey: Godmother of Indian Cooking

Madhur Jaffrey in 1992.

Madhur Jaffrey doesn't call herself a chef. She thinks of herself as a home cook. Other people consider her the godmother of Indian cooking. She is also an award-winning actress, writer, and TV personality.

Jaffrey was born in 1933 in Delhi, India. She studied acting at the Royal Academy of Dramatic Arts in London, England. Jaffrey was there on scholarship, and she didn't have much money. She didn't like the food at the college. Her mother sent her Indian recipes. Jaffrey had never cooked anything before. She hadn't even boiled an egg.

Jaffrey moved to New York in the late 1950s. She started writing articles about food and travel. In 1973, she wrote a cookbook called *An Invitation to Indian Cooking*. Jaffrey's book brought authentic Indian cuisine to America.

Jaffrey has a good palate, and she likes to teach people. In the 1980s, the BBC hired her to work on a show about cooking Indian food. *Madhur*

2004

Year when Madhur Jaffrey was awarded an honorary CBE

- CBE stands for Commander of the Most Excellent Order of the British Empire.
- Jaffrey won the award for her achievements in cultural relations, acting, and cooking.
- In 1994, she won the James Beard Cookbook of the Year Award.

THINK ABOUT IT

Imagine you're in a place where the food is unfamiliar. Would you try to make some of your family favorites? Could you start gathering some family recipes now?

Jaffrey's Indian Cookery was a success. Jaffrey has since written more than 30 cookbooks. Her latest came out in May 2019.

Jaffrey is also known as "the Julia Child of Indian cookery." She was once a guest on Child's cooking show "In Julia's Kitchen." Largely because of her, Indian food is popular in western countries today.

Jaffrey at a signing for one of her cookbooks in 2010.

8

James Beard: Father of American-Style Gourmet Cooking

James Beard in 1949.

Beard wanted to be an actor. He studied in Europe and New York. Backstage, he made dinner for the cast. When his acting career didn't take off, he started a catering company. It was called Hors d'Oeuvre, Inc. Beard earned a reputation as a good cook.

James Beard was born in 1903 in Portland, Oregon. He spent summers at the beach. His family fished, gathered berries, and made meals from what they caught and found.

Beard's first cookbook was published in 1940. It was called *Hors d'Oeuvre & Canapés*. His recipes pulled together simple American and English food. It made Americans aware of their culinary traditions. Beard went on to write more than 20 cookbooks. In 1946, he starred in a live cooking show on NBC called *I Love to Eat*. He was one of the first celebrity chefs on TV.

Beard thought food should be made with fresh, wholesome ingredients. He was an early farm-to-table pioneer. In 1955, he started the James Beard Cooking School. Beard also co-founded Citymeals-on-Wheels, an organization that delivers meals to homebound elderly people in New York City.

In 1986, the year after Beard died, one of his former students started the James Beard Foundation. The first James Beard Awards were given out in May 1991. Today the Beard Awards are known as the Oscars of the food world.

Beard at his book signing in 1981.

50+ million

Number of meals served through Citymeals-on-Wheels since 1981

- During World War II, Beard set up canteens for service people overseas.
- He was a consultant to food and beverage companies.
- In 1973, Beard started teaching a yearly summer cooking class at Seaside High School in Oregon.

THE JAMES BEARD AWARDS

The James Beard Awards are the top honors food and beverage professionals in the United States can receive. Winners take home a certificate and a medallion engraved with the James Beard Foundation symbol.

9

Anthony Bourdain: Bringing Viewers the World

Anthony Bourdain was born in 1956 in New York City. He grew up in a New Jersey suburb. His first restaurant job was as a dishwasher. He often said that job taught him the most important lessons in his life.

2013

Year Anthony Bourdain won a Peabody Award for *Parts Unknown*

- The Peabody honors sensational storytelling from various forms of media.
- Bourdain wrote 13 books during his lifetime, including two crime novels.
- He co-wrote two graphic novels for DC Comics.

Anthony Bourdain after winning his 2016 Emmy.

Bourdain graduated from the Culinary Institute of America in 1978. He worked as a line cook and sous chef and rose through the ranks. In 1998, he became the executive chef at the French restaurant Brasserie Les Halles. In 1999, he wrote an article for the *New Yorker* called "Don't Eat Before Reading

WASTED

A documentary film called *Wasted! The Story of Food Waste* came out in 2017. Anthony Bourdain was the executive producer. More than a billion tons of food are wasted each year around the world. Bourdain hoped that *Wasted!* would help change how people shop, eat, and recycle.

This." It was an honest look at kitchen restaurants. Bourdain's first book, *Kitchen Confidential: Adventures in the Culinary Underbelly*, was published in 2000. It made him a celebrity.

Next, Bourdain became a TV personality. He starred in food and travel series for the Food Network and the Travel Channel. His enthusiastic storytelling drew fans of all ages. His third series, *Anthony Bourdain: Parts Unknown*, aired on CNN. It introduced viewers to eating rituals of cultures all over the world. Bourdain wanted people to see how food bonds people. *Parts Unknown* won six Emmys. Bourdain committed suicide while the 12th season was being filmed. The final episode aired in November 2018.

10

Marcus Samuelsson: Ethiopian Swedish American Chef

Marcus Samuelsson has said that if he weren't a chef, he would have been a soccer player. He was born in Ethiopia in 1971. His mother died in 1973. He was adopted by a Swedish couple named Ann Marie and Lennart Samuelsson and grew up in Sweden. With his new family, Samuelsson went fishing. They caught crayfish and lobster. His grandmother Helga was a professional chef. She taught him how to pickle and preserve food.

Samuelsson attended the Culinary Institute in Gothenburg, Sweden. Later, he emigrated to the United States. In 1994, he was hired by Restaurant Aquavit in New York. He became the youngest chef ever to win a three-star rating from the *New York Times.*

In 2000, Samuelsson returned to Ethiopia and met his biological family. He learned about Ethiopian food and African spices. He wrote a book of recipes and stories called *The Soul of a New Cuisine: A Discovery of Foods and Flavors of Africa.* The James Beard Foundation named it Best International Cookbook in 2007.

Samuelsson doing a cooking segment on *Good Morning America* with First Lady Michelle Obama and anchor Robin Roberts in 2013.

In 2010, Samuelsson opened Red Rooster Harlem in New York. He has since opened more restaurants around the world. *The Red Rooster Cookbook: The Story of Food and Hustle in Harlem* came out in 2016. Samuelsson has been on several cooking shows including *Top Chef Masters* (he won) and *Inner Chef with Marcus Samuelsson*. As host of the PBS show *No Passport Required*, he explored immigrant traditions in American food. He believes in bringing people together around food.

18

Number of siblings Samuelsson has in Ethiopia

- In 2003, the James Beard Foundation named Samuelsson the best chef in New York City.
- In 2009, he was a guest chef at the White House. He planned and ran the first state dinner of the Obama Administration.
- Samuelsson has been a UNICEF Ambassador since 2000.

11

Masaharu Morimoto: Iron Chef

Masaharu Morimoto in 2016.

Masaharu Morimoto was born in Hiroshima, Japan, in 1955. His family was poor. Once a month, they went to a sushi restaurant. Morimoto admired the knife skills of the sushi chefs. He wanted to be a baseball player, but a shoulder injury changed his plans. He learned how to make sushi.

At age 24, Morimoto opened his first restaurant in Hiroshima. He was also interested in Western cooking. At 30, he sold his restaurant and traveled to the United States. Soon he became executive chef at the famous Nobu restaurant in New York City.

Morimoto feels that cooking should be entertainment. During his travels, he learned new ideas that led him to create Japanese-Western fusion food. His cooking uses the bright colors of Japanese dishes and spices from China. It features ingredients from Italian food and presentation from France. Morimoto's food tastes good and looks good.

16

Number of restaurants Masaharu Morimoto owns around the world

- Morimoto only eats one meal a day.
- He doesn't like to cook at home.
- His favorite foods are traditional Japanese vegetarian dishes.

THINK ABOUT IT

Look up the definition of fusion food. What does it mean? Can you think of a time when you ate fusion food? How would you describe the experience?

In 1998, Morimoto competed on a Japanese television show called *Iron Chef*. He caught the attention of the Food Network and became a star on the American version of the show. Morimoto loved showing off his skills to millions of Americans. Viewers loved his fun, creative style.

In 2002, Morimoto opened a restaurant in Philadelphia. He named it Morimoto. He has since opened many more restaurants. His first cookbook, *Morimoto: The New Art of Japanese Cooking,* was published in 2007. It won the Julia Child Award for Best First Book. *Mastering the Art of Japanese Home Cooking* came out in 2016.

Restaurant Morimoto Asia in Orlando, Florida.

12

Jacques Pépin: Legendary Chef

Jacques Pépin is one of the world's most famous and beloved chefs. He was born in Bourg-en-Bresse, France, in 1935. His parents owned the restaurant Le Pelican. Pépin worked in the kitchen with his mother after school. When he was 13, he quit school to become a kitchen apprentice at the Grand Hôtel de l'Europe in his hometown.

One night, when he was still an apprentice, he was called on to cook. The chef had already gone home, but guests had arrived for dinner. He made chicken sautéed in cream and tarragon. The guests were pleased. At age 17, Pépin went to Paris. He worked in many of the city's top restaurants. In his early 20s, he was personal chef to three French presidents.

Pépin moved to the United States in 1959. He settled in New York City. He met chefs Julia Child and James Beard. Years later, he and Child would star together in a cooking series. Pépin would win many James Beard Awards. But before then, in New York, he took a job as director of research for the Howard Johnson hotel and restaurant chain. He flipped burgers and cooked hot dogs. He learned about food chemistry and the culinary tastes of Americans. Meanwhile, he earned two degrees at Columbia University.

Over the years, Pépin has hosted more than a dozen cooking shows on PBS. He has written 29 books including an autobiography. His 16 James Beard Awards include the Lifetime Achievement Award. He has taught countless people new ways to cook and look at recipes. In 1998, Pépin became Dean of Special Programs at the French Culinary Institute. He still teaches and gives food demonstrations today.

2004
Year when Pépin won the Legion of Honor

- The Legion of Honor is France's highest civilian honor.
- Pépin still teaches and gives food demonstrations.
- He loves to paint. He often paints chickens.

Pépin doing a cooking demonstration at the Fabulous Food Show.

More Chefs to Know

Wolfgang Puck

Wolfgang Puck was born in Austria in 1949. He learned how to cook in France. Puck's most famous restaurant is Spago. The name is Italian slang for spaghetti. Puck opened Spago in 1982 on Hollywood's Sunset Strip. The restaurant drew guests for its interesting fusion of French and Italian food. A topping on pizza might include caviar and duck sausage.

Chan Yan-tak

Chan Yan-tak was born in Hong Kong in 1960. After his mother died, he began working in kitchens to help support his family. He rose through the ranks of many Hong Kong restaurants. Today he is the executive chef at the Four Seasons hotel in Hong Kong. Yan-tak learned English through songs like "Are You Lonesome Tonight?" by Elvis Presley. He is the first Chinese chef to earn three Michelin stars.

Rachel Ray

Rachael Ray was born in Glen Falls, New York, in 1968. While working in a gourmet shop in Schenectady, New York, she taught "30 Minute Meals" classes. A local TV station began filming her. The Food Network noticed and offered her a contract. Ray has since hosted several cooking shows. Viewers enjoy her lighthearted approach. Ray teaches them how to take shortcuts in cooking but still make delicious food.

Mashama Bailey

Bailey is the first African-American woman to be nominated for the James Beard Best Chef Award. Bailey was born in New York City. She moved to Savannah, Georgia, to open her restaurant, The Grey. The Grey is in an old Greyhound bus station that used to be segregated. Bailey serves meals that are her own take on Southern food, such as black-eyed pea hummus and foie gras with grits.

Glossary

apprentice
Someone who is learning a trade from a master.

authentic
Genuine or real.

bland
Without strong flavor; not very interesting.

bond
Join together or come together.

canteen
A shop at a military post; a temporary restaurant.

palate
Sense of taste.

patisserie
French cakes and pastries.

pioneer
One of the first; someone who comes up with new ideas and ways of doing things.

presentation
How food is arranged on a plate.

produce
Fruits and vegetables.

sous chef
A chef who's the second-in-command in a kitchen.

traditional
Following customs or behaviors used by a group of people for a long time.

victory garden
A home garden planted during a war, so people could grow their own fruits and vegetables.

Read More

Colella, Jill. *Complete Children's Cookbook: Delicious Step-by-Step Recipes for Young Cooks.* New York: DK Publishing, 2015.

Hammer, Melina. *Kid Chef: The Foodie Kids Cookbook: Healthy Recipes and Culinary Skills for the New Cook in the Kitchen.* Berkeley, CA: Sonoma Press, 2016.

MasterChef Junior Cookbook: Bold Recipes and Essential Techniques to Inspire Young Cooks. New York: Clarkson Potter, 2017.

Index

About the Author

Jamie Kallio is a librarian in the south suburbs of Chicago. She is the author of many nonfiction books for kids. She is not a chef but really enjoys eating food that other people cook.